Amazing You

Psychic Powers

Jessica Adams

h

a division of Hodder Headline Limited

About the series

Amazing You is our stunning new Mind Body Spirit
series. It shows you how to make the most of your life
and boost your chances of success and happiness.
You'll discover some fantastic things about you and
your friends by trying out the great tips and fun
exercises. See for yourself just how amazing you
can be!

Available now
Astrology
Dreams
Numerology
Psychic Powers
Spells

Coming soon
Crystals
Face and Hand Reading
Fortune Telling
Graphology

Acknowledgements

A big thank you to Anne Clark, Belinda Bolliger,
Matt Whyman, Katie Sergeant, Stephanie Cabot,
Fiona Inglis – and to Nick Earls, Helen Basini and
Juliet Partridge, who worked so hard on *Kids' Night In*
while I was beginning to write this book!

About the author

Jessica Adams is a best-selling author, professional astrologer and psychic, who has recently contributed to *Kids' Night In*, in aid of the charity War Child. She has a telepathic ginger cat called Henry and lives between her homes in Brighton, England and Bellingen, Australia.

For free Star Sign screensavers and e-cards and more *Amazing You* fun, visit **www.jessicaadams.com**. Jessica has also written *Astrology* in the *Amazing You* series.

Text copyright © Jessica Adams 2004
Illustrations copyright © Jo Quinn/Inkshed.co.uk 2004
Cover illustration © Monica Laita 2004

Editor: Katie Sergeant
Book design by Don Martin
Cover design: Hodder Children's Books

Published in Great Britain in 2004
by Hodder Children's Books

A catalogue record for this book is available from the British Library.

10 9 8 7 6 5 4 3 2 1

ISBN: 0340882050

Printed and bound by Bookmarque Ltd, Croydon, Surrey

The paper and board used in this paperback by Hodder Children's Books
are natural recyclable products made from wood grown in sustainable
forests. The manufacturing processes conform to the environmental
regulations of the country of origin.

Hodder Children's Books
a division of Hodder Headline Limited
338 Euston Road, London NW1 3BH

Contents

Introduction

If you've ever had a dream about a future event which came true, or accurately guessed a fact about someone you could not have known, then you may be using your psychic skills without even realizing it! Intuition can help you at school, with your family, with friends, with boys, and even on your holidays. It can also help you understand your pets. But most of all it's a great way of finding out more about amazing YOU.

You'll learn lots of fantastic psychic techniques in this book, but don't get too carried away. Practise the exercises sensibly and have fun. Always remember that you're in control of your life and have the power to shape your future. Use your psychic gift for the good of all – and your powers will grow stronger. The more practical you are the better a psychic you will be. Are you ready to switch on your psychic powers? Just turn the page ...

CHAPTER ONE

Mind-reading

Everyone is psychic, which means we all have the ability to guess who's on the telephone, call our cat or dog for breakfast without having to speak, and even predict the future. You'll find out how to do all this, and more, in this book.

With practice, this natural psychic ability can be trained, so that it's possible to read your best friend's mind, or even do things like find lost objects. Are some people more psychic than others? Of course. Some girls are better at sport than you, or better at music, maths or essays. It's the same with psychic ability. But all of us can run across a field, play a note on the recorder, add 2 + 2 or write a sentence. Psychic aptitude is a bit like this. It's a natural ability which can exist in small ways or big ways – but it still exists!

Practise, practise, practise!

Think of this book as your psychic gym, which will help you train your psychic muscles. Throughout the book you'll be given the equivalent of push-ups, or sit-ups, using your psychic self. If you do these exercises daily, you should find your sixth sense becomes powerful pretty quickly.

Here's your first psychic exercise. Can you sense when someone is staring at your back?

If you catch buses a lot, perhaps you've already discovered one important part of your psychic ability. It's called sensing, and the famous English scientist, Rupert Sheldrake, has discovered that most people can do it – especially if they are being stared at.

Is there a boy you like sitting a few rows behind you on the bus, gazing at you? Your psychic ability will allow you to 'feel' it – and I bet that if you turn around quickly, you'll catch him staring at you. You can't see or hear someone staring at you from the side, or behind you, but you'll probably have a funny feeling that they are – and you'll be right.

★ ★ TRY IT ON THE BUS!

Next time you catch the bus, get on the top deck next to a window, or if the bus only has one deck, make sure you sit right at the back, next to a window. The idea is to give yourself a good view of people in the street, without them noticing you.

Look around at the crowds walking past the bus. Pick one particular person. It could be a grand-motherly type, or a businessman, or another kid about your age. Start staring at them. Remember, they can't see you, but you must definitely be able to see them (this is why a double-decker bus is so useful for this experiment). Watch what happens. In a few moments, this person will turn and stare back at the bus, or even stare straight through the window where you happen to be sitting. Our psychic ability gives us the power to know when we are being stared at!

★★ RING, RING – WHO'S THERE?

Rupert Sheldrake has also successfully tested people's ability to know who is on the other end of the phone before picking it up. This psychic skill seems to work well if the other person is a member of your family, or a good friend, or a boyfriend. If you like, you can try an experiment to see this for yourself. Ask someone to be the experimenter, and make sure they have a dice. Give the experimenter the names and numbers of six really good friends. (They'll have to be in on the experiment too, or it won't work!)

You should use a landline phone and not your mobile because you can see who's calling on your mobile screen. Arrange to be near the phone at a certain time – preferably on a day when it won't drive your Mum or Dad mad to have constant calls coming in. And remember to ask for

permission to do this experiment from the adult
who pays the bill. Then get your experimenter to
give each friend a dice number: 1, 2, 3, 4, 5 or 6.
The dice is thrown six times.

Each time the experimenter
throws the dice and gets a number,
he or she calls the friend whose
number it is. If the experimenter
throws the same number four or even five times
in row, then that poor friend will have to make
four or five calls to you!

Six times in an hour, you will receive six calls.
As the phone is ringing, concentrate hard on who
might be on the other end. Can you see a picture
of their face in your mind's eye? Do you just
KNOW who it is? Have you heard their name
almost spoken in your imagination? If you turn
out to be right, even just once, congratulations –
you are showing strong psychic skills.

To make sure the test is fair, you might want
to ask a witness to watch you write down the
names of each caller on a sheet before you pick
up the phone, so that everyone has proof that
you really were right. Or you could video yourself
hearing the phone ring, writing down the name of

the person you anticipate, and then picking it up.
Get the person who was throwing the dice (the
experiment controller) to ring everyone up at the
end and check out the scores. Are you psychic?
This is a good way to find out if you are!

These two experiments are quick and easy versions
of more serious experiments set up by Rupert
Sheldrake in his book, *The Sense of Being Stared
At.* If you are curious about setting up a proper
scientific study of your psychic powers (and your
friends') then the book will show you how, or you
can visit **www.sheldrake.org** for more information.
Who knows, you might be able to prove
something that changes the face of science!

⋆⋆ GETTING IT WRONG

If this is your first attempt at psychic stuff, it's
quite likely that you'll get a few calls wrong. And
maybe staring at a poor old granny on the other
side of the street won't make her look up. But
don't let that put you off. Research proves that

6

people are most psychic when they are feeling relaxed and quietly confident about what they can do. So don't tell yourself that you're a rubbish psychic; instead, concentrate on what you got right. You can always try again another day.

What sort of psychic are you?

To find out what kind of psychic you are, you need to discover which of the 'clairs' you are in the family, as you may be clairvoyant, clairaudient, clairsentient or even clairfragrant. Where your phone experiment is concerned, this is very important. Try to remember how you knew who would be on the other end of the phone. If you saw a picture of them in your mind's eye, then you may be clairvoyant. If you heard a little voice inside your head saying their name, then you may be clairaudient (if you heard their voice as well, you will also be clairaudient). What about if you smelled the perfume or shampoo they always use? Then you are clairfragrant, although this is

7

unusual. And if you just KNEW who it was? Then you are clairsentient. Professional psychics can use all the different abilities at once in their work, so they are seeing, hearing, knowing and smelling all at the same time.

★★ THE AMAZING MIND-READING EXPERIMENT

Now that you've tried a couple of psychic exercises and experiments, you are ready to read minds. Don't worry – it's not hard. But it's not a trick either! The most important thing is that you do it with people you know and really like. So if you are fighting with your sister this week, don't ask her. And don't bother with people you only know slightly. The very best mind-reading results come from working with friends, boys or family members who you see regularly and usually have fun with.

Now find ten objects

You will both need to find five ordinary household objects, which you then put into a big black rubbish bag, or some other kind of bag, like a hessian sack, which is large enough to hold everything, but impossible to see through.

Ask permission from your parents first, because they need to know what you're doing (otherwise they might wonder what happened to the paint they had in the shed, when you put it in your bag). But do be clever about what you pick up and hide. A toothbrush is a bit obvious, but how about the goldfish food? Try to work one room ahead of each other too, so that you're not accidentally seeing each other. Don't try to be clever and guess what the other person is choosing to put in the bag either – it might not be what you think, and your logic will also get in the way of your mind-reading ability.

Your turn first

How good are you at telepathic sending? In other words, how good are you at closing your eyes, and sending a picture in your mind's eye? This is the first test for you both. The other person will need a piece of paper and a pen, and have to sit in another room with the door closed while you do it. Have a watch or clock handy. You are going to take ten minutes to do this – in other words, one minute per object. Are you ready? Then sort through the bag and pick up one object, and using your mind, SEND! Your partner is allowed to write down what he/she thinks the object is, but also to draw it if they are seeing a picture or a shape. Remember to make a list at your end as well, so you both get things in order. Number it 1 to 10, in order of the different objects that you are sending.

Tips for successful sending

Try to use all your 'clair' senses to get your message across. So smell the object. See it in your mind. 'Say' the name of the object in your mind.

The more you bombard the other person with lots of different ways of getting the message across, the easier it will be for him/her to read your mind. Be quick though. If you try too hard you will wear yourself out. And as people usually 'receive' very quickly, you don't need more than a minute to send each object, each time.

Sending an orange

As an example, here's a super-successful psychic way to send an orange. First of all, see it in your imagination. Then 'feel' it by mentally touching it with your fingers, so that you can sense its roughness. Now taste it – you should be able to imagine the spicy-sweet taste. Feel the juiciness too! And smell it. It's a very sharp, bright smell isn't it? Finally, practise saying the word 'orange' in your mind. You might even want to say your partner's name first, and then the name of the fruit. So you could close your eyes in the other room and send this message: 'GEORGIA it's an ORANGE!'

So, how did you do?

After ten minutes, check your partner's piece of paper. How close were they? Sometimes, when people do this mind-reading test for the first time, they often get the objects right but in the wrong order. And they can also almost get things right – like saying 'fruit', for example, instead of 'orange' – but remember that psychics always do better when they are feeling relaxed. So even if your partner only got one thing right, or none at all, don't take it too seriously. Treat it as a fun experiment. The more fun you have, the better your results will gradually be.

Tips for successful receiving

Now it's your turn to receive. So, with the door closed, relax in a nice, comfortable position and have your eyes closed, waiting to get the psychic post from your partner in the other room. Don't try too hard. And if you change your mind about what you think the object is, feel free to cross it out and start again. Try to imagine that your head is empty, waiting

for something to pop in. Don't distract yourself by trying to remember if you fed the cat this morning, or worrying about what you're going to wear on Saturday. Just relax and keep your mind nice and open, like an empty postbox.
Allow one minute for every object, and if you want to do drawings as well as make notes, then do that too.

Repeating the experiment

The more you repeat this experiment with each other, the better you should get, until you are at the stage where you can send and receive all sorts of different messages. Instead of doing objects, you might be able to send whole sentences. Two girls I know, Lucy and Charlotte, did this quite well one day when Lucy got lost in the shopping centre, buying some stripey socks! Charlotte had forgotten to take her mobile phone with her, and although she looked for ages, she couldn't find her friend anywhere. Sitting down on a bench, she decided to have an ice cream, stop worrying, and wait. While she was relaxed, she had a very strong message pop into her head about Lucy being at the front of the building. Sure enough, when she checked at the front of the shopping centre, this is exactly where her friend was – by the doors. In her panic, Lucy had 'sent' Charlotte a message about her whereabouts. Because the two friends often did fun telepathy mind-reading experiments together, they had become skilled at reading each other's minds!

★★ THE POWER OF TWO!

If you and your friend become good at reading minds, you might like to practise reading lives. You do this by holding someone's watch or ring in your hand (preferably someone you don't know very well) and telling them about their past. A relative you haven't seen for a while is a good guinea pig for this kind of experiment, or even your friend's Mum or Dad. As you hold their jewellery try and use one of your 'clair' senses

to pick up facts about their childhood
or teenage years. Were they a dancer?
Did they break their arm when they
were little? Were they good at maths?
With practice, you and your friend
might be able to pick up an amazing amount
of secret knowledge about other people, just by
tuning into their jewellery. This method works
because their aura, or energy field, is attached
to what they wear. For more on this and some
fascinating facts about colour energy, turn to
Chapter five.

The most important rule in mind-reading is
to relax and have fun as when you're happy and
chilled out you're more likely to pick up on
psychic vibes. So now that you've tried reading
human minds it's time to extend your psychic
powers to reading animals' minds. Read on to
find out more!

CHAPTER TWO

Amazing psychic pets

So far so good. You've seen lots of ways in which human beings like you can be psychic. But what about animals? If you've ever had a clever cat or dog, you'll know that they can anticipate feeding time – even when you're late or early with the food – and also that they can tell when you're coming home. The scientist, Rupert Sheldrake, who did the experiments with people staring at each others' backs, has done some amazing studies on dogs that can tell when their owners are coming home, so it's not just your mutt! Psychic pets are actually quite common.

Be a cat whisperer

I have read the minds of both cats and dogs, and I find cats easier because they are less bouncy and excitable, and calmer to talk to. You can do it too. You need to wait for a time when your cat is in a cuddly mood though. It's no good doing this when they are yowling for food, or are busy eating, or are just fast asleep. You need to read their minds when they are relaxed and alert, so that their psychic abilities will be stronger.

★★ AM I MAKING IT UP?

How do you know that you aren't making it up? The answer is, you won't. But some things your cat tells you will just seem right. Look into their eyes, and silently ask them if there's anything they'd like to tell you. Let them know that they have a safe and happy home with you, and that you are very happy you are together ... BUT ... is there anything they want to say?

Close your eyes, tune in and listen. You will be amazed at the results! Some cats talk about their food. Some cats talk about the way they are put out at night. Other animals just want to say, 'This is my chair', or even, 'Thank you.'

I once looked after a house where there was a huge, old, very fluffy cat called Jackson. His owners, Wendy and Jeremy, were away, and I had been left to feed him while I stayed in the house. Jackson was a very proud cat, with big golden eyes and a definite attitude. Nevertheless, I tuned into him psychically, to see if there was anything he wanted to tell me. There was. He said, loud and clear in my mind, 'Welcome to MY house!' And that's the way he wanted to keep it ...

Psychic dogs

If you really want to see psychic dogs in action, set up a video camera on a tripod with an hour-long tape in it. If you don't have a video camera you could perhaps borrow one from a friend, or even from your school if you explain what it's for and ask permission. Make sure everyone leaves the house, so your dog is left alone. Then come back at a time that your dog would not be expecting. In other words, if you normally leave at breakfast and come home at dinner, why not try coming home an hour or two early? If it's the weekend, you could leave, go out for twenty minutes, then come straight back home. What you are watching for on the video, though, is a sign that your dog is being excitable and acting strangely – going to the window, whining at the door, or running around. These are all signs that your dog knows you are coming home. And HOW does he know it? Because he is psychic! Rupert Sheldrake calls it their extra sense.

20

⋆⋆ AMAZING YOU AND YOUR AMAZING PETS

The more psychic you are, the more psychic your pets will become. They will sense that you can speak 'their' language and you may even find that they can warn you of really useful things, like bad storms, or even fires. On an everyday level, though, it's just nice to chat. If you ever thought cats and dogs were dumb animals, think again. They know exactly what's going on in your flat or house, and they even know what's happening with your family! Some psychics have even become professional pet psychics these days, so that they can come round to your place and sort out animals' problems (for example, if they are off their food and drink). Pet psychics can even work with racehorses, to see why they're not racing as well as they used to ... sometimes the answers surprise even the owners!

✦✶ WHY PSYCHICS LOVE THEIR PETS

Professional psychics, like me, love their pets, because they are good 'practice animals' for every day. If you build a special relationship with your cat, dog – even your fish or budgie – then you can get into the habit of practising telepathy every day too. My cat Henry has even learned how to use a cat telephone! When I am far away from home, he telepathically tells other ginger cats like him to stand in my way, or jump in my path, so they can meow a message to me. Whenever this happens, I always know to call the neighbour who is feeding and looking after Henry – and sure enough, he always needs to go to the vet, or a new flea collar, or a change of cat food.

Does your cat know how to use a cat telephone? If you are away from home on holiday, see for yourself. Chances are if your moggy wants to get a message through to you, he or she will find a way of letting you know!

CHAPTER THREE

Seeing the future

Psychic games

If you have *Monopoly* or *Scrabble* then you can do a very simple psychic test which will help you and your friends see into the future. You can do it with one other person, or in a group – but the important thing is that everyone has a piece of paper and a pen.

As you know, *Monopoly* and *Scrabble* are games of chance. In *Monopoly*, nobody knows what property they're going to land on next, or which card they're going to pick up from

Community Chest. Nobody even knows if they're going to end up in jail! *Scrabble* is also mysterious. When you pick up letters

from the bag, you're never quite sure what you're going to get.

With this test, there is a game within a game – and it's a psychic game. Stop play, and ask everyone to write down the following.

If it's *Monopoly*, ask them to write down: which property the dice will land on in the very last throw of the game; and when the next player has his or her turn, where will he or she end up? Next, write down who you think the winner of the game will be. Be careful! It might not be who you think it's going to be. *Monopoly* is a game where even someone who has lots of properties and money saved up can sometimes lose in the end.

And write down the property you think will have the most hotels on it at the end of the game. Once again, it might not be the place you think. Just because somewhere has two hotels on it now, doesn't mean it's going to have them later. Exercise those psychic powers!

What you are doing with this test is seeing into the near future and it's very likely that you, or one of your friends, will get accurate results.

And the more you play and practise, the more psychic you will become.

With *Scrabbble*, it's simple. Try and use your clairvoyant (clear seeing), clairaudient (clear hearing) or clairsentient (clear knowing) ability to work out which words will end up on the board at the end of the game. Once again, this is a test of your psychic abilities, not your logic. Your common sense might tell you that because there are a lot of words on the board with 'z' in them, that at the end of the game, you might end up  with 'zebra' or 'zealous' or 'pizza'! But anything can happen in a game of *Scrabble*. So switch off your logic and start using your psychic powers. Which five words, not on the board now, will be there at the very end of the game? Keep it a secret until the very end, when you can look at each other's results.

★★ CURIOUS *SCRABBLE* RESULTS

There is a chance you will get some curious *Scrabble* results, even if you really are being a super psychic. For example, you might not guess the actual five words on the board at the end of the game, but you might guess their meaning! Here's an example.

Georgia's mad Psychic Scrabble

Georgia and her three friends, Felix, Alexander and Phoebe, were all playing *Scrabble* and guessing which five words would be on the board at the end of the game that weren't there now.

Georgia guessed: orange, banana, staircase, friends, goat

Felix guessed: apple, supermarket, home, gorilla, circle

Alexander guessed: doctor, dentist, lift, carpet, crying

28

Phoebe guessed: snake, bathroom, pain,
mother, fur

Hardly any of these words ended up on the board at the end of the game, but there were several words that had something in common with the lists.

✳ HEALTH was one of them. This makes Georgia think of eating fruit, and Felix think of apples in big supermarket bags. It makes Alexander think of doctors and dentists, and Phoebe think of pain! (She had just been to hospital.)

✳ HOME was one of them too – so Felix was right. But Georgia guessed staircase (her house has a big staircase), and Alexander guessed carpet and lift (his block of flats has a lift and new carpet in the hall), and Phoebe guessed bathroom and mother (when she is at home, her mother likes to spend lots of time in the bath!).

✳ ZOO was also on the board at the end of the game. This might explain why Georgia thought of a goat, Felix guessed a gorilla, and Phoebe guessed snake and fur. But why did Alexander also guess crying? He said it was because animals locked up in cages in zoos always made him want to cry!

This wasn't a bad result for a first game. There were at least three words on the board at the end of the *Scrabble* match that had quite a lot to do with what the friends were guessing – and Felix even got one exactly right.

Try it yourself. It's a way of playing an extra game with yourself while the real game is going on. And if you practise and have fun, you will be developing your psychic skills all the time.

⋆⋆ REMEMBER – NO CHEATING!

You can't cheat with Psychic *Scrabble* or Psychic *Monopoly.* You must keep your predictions secret until the very end of the game, otherwise there's a chance that you or your friends might deliberately try to make the psychic guesses come true. (For example, if you write down that the property with the most hotels at the end of the game is going to be Park Lane, you might deliberately buy it, and put hotels on it, so that it all comes true!) For super security, you might even want to give your sheets of paper to your Mum or Dad to look after until the end.

Now that you have had some fun exercising your psychic muscles on the bus (use the bus as a mobile psychic gym), or with the phone, or with your favourite board games, you can try something harder – seeing tomorrow's news today.

★★★
Can you see tomorrow's news today?

Psychics believe that there is no real time – in other words, there is no such thing as the true past, present and future. If you have ever flown in an aeroplane and crossed the international date line, you'll know this is true. How can it be yesterday in Los Angeles when it's tomorrow in Australia but the clock and calendar on the aeroplane says it is? Einstein believed that if astronauts travelled fast enough into space, they would age differently from the people they had left behind on Earth. Many scientists say that time is something we've made up to keep life nice and organised, but in actual fact, the future has already happened, which is why it's so easy to see it!

★★ PSYCHIC TV NEWS

Seeing tomorrow's news today is something you can test yourself with – you won't need your friends, although if you start getting lots of accurate results, perhaps you'd like to get them to witness your experiments later on.

Start by lying down on your bed at home. Make sure you're not too hot and not too cold, and stick a 'Do Not Disturb' sign on the door. Make sure people know you're not to be interrupted for half an hour.

It helps to have your shoes off, and not too many tight clothes on, just so you feel relaxed – though don't get so comfortable that you fall asleep!

Squeeze your toes really tightly, count to five, then let them go. Next, squeeze your bottom, count to five, then breathe out and relax. Next, pull your arms in really tightly to your sides, as if you had chicken wings. Hold them for the count of five, then aaaah! let them go, and flop out again. Finally, screw up your face really tightly for the count of five, then relax.

Enjoy the sensation of feeling loose and floaty, and start noticing the way you are breathing. Could you make it slower? Could you make it deeper, so that you're making a slight whistling or breathing sound through your nose? (I'm betting that you'll be breathing through your nose, not your mouth, at this stage – because it's what you do when you are most deeply relaxed.)

 Now, imagine your TV set. See it in your mind's eye. Watch it switch on to the station that the family normally watches the news on. See the usual newsreader who's on in the evenings. What are they wearing? Can you see colours, or even jewellery? Now, most importantly, try to hear, see or sense what they are saying. There are usually three or four big news stories at the beginning of the news – stories that everyone pays attention to. What are you picking up, as you visualize the TV set? Remember, it's tomorrow's news today.

Try to get a feeling for the FEELINGS you have about the news story you are seeing, hearing or sensing. Does it make you laugh, does it make you sad, upset or even angry? Do you understand what's going on, or does it confuse you? Put your common sense aside. Don't try to guess the news, just because you read the paper today and think you can predict what is coming next. The most amazing psychic results come from feeling and sensing, not from using your logic.

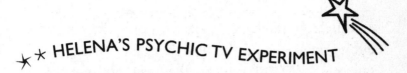

✦✦ HELENA'S PSYCHIC TV EXPERIMENT

Helena had to stop herself falling asleep on her bed two or three times when she tried seeing tomorrow's news today, because she was so relaxed! In the end, though, it was worth it. This is what Helena saw:

- ✹ 'The newsreader is a man tonight. He's got a blue tie.'
- ✹ 'Something about sheep on a boat.'
- ✹ 'Lots of people swimming in the sea.'
- ✹ 'Football! And I felt really excited about it, as if I wanted to get my brother to watch.'

Helena wrote down everything she thought, felt and saw while she was lying on the bed. (Remember to keep a pen and paper handy so you can do this too.) Then she waited a whole night and day, to see if her psychic TV prediction had been right.

What happened next?

As usual, the family sat down to watch the news during dinner – and the first thing that Helena saw was a WOMAN reading the news, and not the man she had pictured. But she *was* wearing a blue jacket, so Helena gave herself some psychic points for guessing the colour.

The first story was about sheep being stuck on a boat in the middle of the ocean. Helena was amazed!

Next came two news reports Helena had not seen, but soon the weather forecast came on. Because it had been an unusually hot day, the weatherman showed pictures of people spending the afternoon on the beach, so Helena was right. She had seen lots of people swimming in the sea after all.

Finally, football. Well – that's on almost every night. But what was interesting about Helena's prediction was the strong feeling of excitement that she got from watching it on her Psychic TV, and the urge she felt to go and get her brother.

As it turned out, she was right. A news report showed her favourite team (and her brother's) scoring a fantastic goal. And just as she had in her experiment 24 hours before, Helena ran out of the room to get her brother and tell him!

✦✧ NEXT MONTH'S NEWS!

Once you have a little more practice predicting tomorrow night's news, start predicting next month's. If it's July 10th today, what do you think will be happening in the world on August 10th? Do the relaxation exercise you learned before, and make sure you write everything down. Then, get a friend or a member of your family to watch you putting it in an envelope and sealing it safely inside. Keep the envelope in a safe place, then on the night of your prediction, open it up and see what you got.

✦✧✦ ✧ ✱ ✧ ⅄
✱ ✧
✦ ✧

Happy news!

If you like, you can make an agreement with yourself to only see happy news. (Otherwise it can be a bit depressing!) In a month from now, will there be a news story that makes you smile or laugh? If you like, you can also try this experiment with a newspaper, as well as the TV news. When you are doing your psychic relaxation exercise, make sure you visualize the normal paper that your Mum or Dad gets every day. Instead of seeing TV pictures this time, see if you can visualize photographs, headlines and even whole stories. Or do you just 'know' what they are going to be? Write it all down and seal it in an envelope.

✶✶ STRANGE BUT TRUE

Research on professional psychics has shown that they make accurate predictions when they are personally involved with a news story, or feel very strong emotions about it. If the psychics are not interested, or feel the news is boring, they won't be so successful. Here's an example. If there is a news story about your school next month, we can bet that you'll predict it more easily than a story about politicians in a place you've never heard of. Or if there's a really funny news story about an escaped pig, the chances are higher that you'll predict it. If you really care about football – and maybe about just one player, like David Beckham – then it's likely that you'll be able to make quite good predictions about him. So try to predict news stories you think you'll be interested in – and it's more likely they'll come to pass.

Predictions for the year 2050!

I'm a professional psychic, so I have to make predictions all the time. The hardest thing I ever got asked was to predict the year 2050 though – mainly because I'll probably be gone by then! Read what I came up with, and then come up with some predictions of your own. If you send them to me at **jessicacadams@aol.com**, I'll gather them all together. Who knows, if your predictions appear on my website, they might even become cyberspace legends – even if you are a little old lady when they finally come true. So here are my predictions:

Clothes

Clothes that make men and women look the same are coming into fashion in the 21st century. As the planet Neptune moves through the sci-fi sign of Aquarius, we will see special outfits with electronic chips in them that tell the police your name, age, address and even your blood group.

Hair

Don't worry if your dad is a baldie, because they will invent amazing new ways for bald men to grow their hair back in the next 20 years. Long hair will be out of fashion though, unless you tie it up in weird and wonderful new ways.

Talking gloves

Special gloves, which have tiny mobile phone technology in them, mean you'll be able to talk into your hand soon – and have a conversation with your friend up the road. A special keypad in the palm of your hand will let you type in a number.

Coloured underwear

You can buy coloured underwear now, of course, but in the future all the colours will have healing properties as well. So you might buy a bright green vest if you want to feel happier, or you might buy some flaming red knickers to get more energy.

No more money!

So much for saving up your coins in a jam jar. In the Age of Aquarius, we won't have money any more – just artificial money, kept in a big world bank. You will have a special identity chip that you use to pay for everything – even your magazines.

New email language

A new email language, similar to texting, will be developed, so that people can get their message across very quickly. There will be a new code of symbols and pictures that lets people know you'll be home for tea, for example.

New mobile sounds

Tiny phones that are built into gloves will be fashionable, but the old phones will still be around too – although they will be extremely small. They will transmit sound signals that also have a special meaning. A sharp 'wheee' sound will mean you're running late.

Super homes

Marriage and having families won't be so popular in the Age of Aquarius. So people don't get lonely, there will be new super homes built, in super villages, where everyone shares the same big dining room so they can eat together.

Connecting with your ancestors

Special machines that allow you to say 'hello' to your ancestors will be invented. They will be very expensive at first, but in time lots of people will be able to use them. You'll be able to talk to your great-great-great grandad's 'ghost'!

Group thinking – a new way to think?

Aquarius rules groups, and these groups can be enormous, and span many countries. Don't be too surprised if you get into one of these huge groups – they might be called something like People Families – in the future. What this means is, a whole group of children who are about your age, with your interests, likes and dislikes, will regularly get together on the Internet to solve problems and ask questions together. Normally, you might go and ask your parents, or a teacher, or just try and work things out for yourself. However, group thinking will be a popular new way of sorting your life out.

NOW – WHAT ABOUT YOUR PREDICTIONS?

Send your predictions to **jessicacadams@aol.com** and I'll put the best ones up on my website. If you'd like to do some more psychic gym exercises, let me know when you write and I can put them up on the site for you too ...

Using your psychic powers to predict the future is a fantastic way to see what exciting things are ahead. Have some fun with your friends and see what you come up with. That said, always remember that predictions are not set in stone and that you have choices and free will to decide what is best for you. Approach the psychic arts with a sensible mind and good judgement and you'll be all the more powerful for it.

CHAPTER FOUR

What's your Life's Fate?

Fate and free will

Psychics believe that some things about the future are fated – they're going to happen, no matter what anyone does. However, they also believe that other bits of the future are subject to free will. In other words, almost anything could happen, and you are free to decide what goes on. When you are predicting tomorrow's news today, you are seeing the fated bits of the future, not the free will bits. Free will is all about CHOOSING, so it's harder to see. It's the 'fate' bits that are much easier to predict, because they're already going to happen ...

For example, it might be your fate to get married to a man in another country. One way or another, that's going to happen to you – and you'll be so madly in love with him you won't be able to say no! But what about the free will bits? These might involve the jobs you have along the way. To find this man, perhaps you'll need to become a flight attendant, so you can end up in the country where he lives. Or maybe you'll buy a lottery ticket and win enough money to take a holiday there. Or you might even take a job as a nurse, so you work in a hospital in his country. THOSE are the choice bits and the free will bits. But the fate part of it is meeting the man and marrying him. That's something that was always, always going to happen. And nine times out of ten, that's what a psychic person sees.

What's your Life's Fate?

Everyone is born with a special mission, or fate, to complete. Before the age of 16 you have a much better chance of knowing what this is. Did you know that famous musicians like Mozart or Paul McCartney were mad about music when they were kids? They knew their fate while they were very young. As you grow older, it can be harder to remember what your mission is meant to be, which is why it's a good idea to do this experiment now. For extra amazement, do it with your closest friends, or brothers and sisters. The chances are, by using your combined brain power, you should all be able to psychically see your Life's Fate!

★★ THE RULES

The rules are simple. When you predict your Life's Fate for yourself, and for others in the group, it has to be something that comes from your psychic self, not necessarily your common sense. Let's say your best friend is good at maths and she's always saying she wants to be a vet. Perhaps you think it's her Life's Fate to be a vet – but remember, it might not be! The only way to tell is to use your psychic skills. Perhaps the true answer about her Life's Fate will really surprise you when you do. And what is she predicting for you? Is it something that most people might have known or guessed, or is it something quite unexpected?

★★ HOW TO DO THE EXPERIMENT

Make sure you all have pens and paper – up to eight good friends or close brothers and sisters (and cousins!) can do this experiment.

Get comfortable on the floor – sitting down or
lying on the rug is much better than sitting up
in chairs. Make it a rule that nobody is laughing
or talking when you do this experiment either.
You all need to concentrate quite hard to get it
right. And remember – put up your 'Do Not
Disturb' sign on the door, or just ask other people
to give you half an hour of peace and quiet for
the experiment.

Step one

Now everyone is comfortable, get someone to
say this aloud: 'Dear Universe, please assist us
to predict our Life's Fate. What are we here to do
in this lifetime? Everyone is here to help everyone
else on this planet. How will each of us help?'

Step two

Read this aloud: 'Will everyone in this room
please imagine themselves surrounded by
white light, and ask to know their own and their
friends' Life's Fate, for the highest good of all.'
(The person reading aloud should also surround
themselves with white light.)

Step three

Read this aloud: 'Now, relax, close your eyes, and allow yourself to see, hear or know your Life's Fate. If it doesn't make sense, don't worry. Write it down anyway.'

Step four

Now say: 'Write down your name next to your Life's Fate, and the date. Now, fold the piece of paper under so nobody can see what's written on it, then pass the piece of paper to the person on your right, and get them to write down YOUR Life's Fate on it, with their name alongside it.'

Step five

Repeat this process (including the folding) until everyone has a piece of paper with Life's Fate predictions on it. There should be the original prediction you wrote for yourself, with your name next to it, at the top. Then beneath this, there will be Life's Fate predictions for you, folded under every time, by each of your friends.

Example

Twenty years ago, Rachel did a Life's Fate experiment with her sister, Jemima, and her two friends, Pippa and Emma. They were 12 years old, and trying to see what their Life's Fate would be.

Rachel's prediction for herself was that she would teach children how to balance.

Jemima's prediction for Rachel was that she would help people who were lost.

Pippa's prediction for Rachel was that she would have a little boy called Arthur.

Emma's prediction for Rachel was that she would have two children.

Some fascinating things came to pass in Rachel's life by the time she was 32. She became a PE teacher in a large school for girls and boys, and two of her subjects were orienteering (which teaches people how to find their way with a compass) and gymnastics (which involves balance).

53

She had a little boy, and his name was Marcus, not Arthur, but funnily enough Rachel said her husband had been brought up with a goldfish called Arthur, so Pippa was almost right. And will she go on to have two children in the end? All Emma can do is wait and see!

By the way, Rachel's predictions for her sister, and her friends, weren't quite as good as other people's for her. But that happens too. The main thing is, to try and have fun with the experiment. If you really want to amaze yourselves, put the answers in a sealed envelope, in a safe place (free from silverfish or moths) and try to keep it for the next 20 years. Then you can get everyone together again and open it to see whether your predictions came true.

More on your Life's Fate

So how is our Life's Fate decided? Many psychics believe we actually decide it before we are born. When we are just souls or spirits, waiting to find a body, we decide what sorts of things we'd like to do in our lives, and even the people we'd like to be friends with, or have in our family, or go out with. Our choices are ruled by a desire to make progress. In other words, we want lives that will teach us, and help us, and help other people too. Before we are born, we set out the really big, important things about our future lives – also known as fate – and then with the help of free will, we set about fulfilling what we came here to do.

THE GOLDEN PSYCHIC RULE

No matter if you are doing the Life's Fate experiment, or anything else in this book, you must remember the golden psychic rule, which is very simple. **Always do what you do for the highest good of all.** In fact, you might even like to say it out loud before you do any kind of psychic stuff: 'I'm doing this for the highest good of all.' Another simple way to say this is, 'Help me to help others and help myself.'

Amazingly, when you say this, your psychic ability seems to become even more powerful. The most successful professional psychics are people who spend a lot of their time doing anything from finding lost dogs, to helping people get over the sadness of somebody dying. And they can also do practical things, like help people get great jobs! Psychics who are here to serve are often the most accurate of all.

⋆⋆ MAKING WISHES COME TRUE!

Some of the wonderful things about your Life's Fate are just within reach ... but you'll never know if you don't reach out for them. Making wishes come true is a remarkable ability that some lucky people seem to be born with. But is it luck, or do they just have a better understanding of their Life's Fate?

If you can picture a road map for a moment, with one main red road going through lots of other little roads, avenues and cul-de-sacs, you will get a better idea of what your Life's Fate looks like to a professional psychic. People who get paid to see the future for a living can also see your past and present – just like a road map. Do you want to go to Australia for a holiday, or have a fantastic job in TV when you leave school, or win an award for your painting, or come first in the school swimming gala?

Sometimes your wishes are closer than you think, but because you get lazy (or even worse, don't think your wishes can ever come true) you never try ... and you zoom straight past the avenue or street on your 'road map' which might have led to your secret wishes.

See the map and make a wish

Close your eyes for a minute, and think about
some of your biggest hopes, wishes and dreams.
I bet you've got at least ten of them,
so let yourself spend quite a bit of
time focusing on what you long for
(or who you long for!).

Believe it or not, at least one of these wishes
will be weeks, months or even just a year or two
away. So take a few deep breaths and ask your
higher self to let you know which one is so close
you could touch it. Keep your mind blank for a
few seconds, and just wait to see what you think
of first.

What did you see?

Trust your higher self! Now that you have done
lots of psychic exercises in this book you should
be strongly tuned into tomorrow – and your
personal road map of destiny. So when you see,
hear or 'know' exactly which wish you can make
come true, make sure you chase it as hard as you
can. Did you see a pair of ballet shoes? Maybe

your ballet lessons are closer than you think. Did you see a boy that you've had a crush on for ages? Your higher self is telling you that a special time with him could be well within your reach.

Feel it, see it, make it happen

Now that you know you're not going to bypass the road that leads to your innermost wish (you never knew it was so close, did you?) there are ways you can make sure it comes true for you. If your higher self has told you that you really CAN make it into the school diving team, for example, find a notebook that has plenty of space to draw in, or glue pictures into, and make that a book that you dedicate to your wish. Draw yourself diving, in front of an admiring crowd. Cut out pictures of Olympic medallists in the pool, astonishing the judges, and glue them in. You get the idea! Now you know which of your ten wishes is just around the corner, try to pour masses of energy into it by building a special 'dreams come true' book around it.

✶✶ WISH BOOKS REALLY WORK!

I have used wish books (and so have my friends) since I was quite young, and believe it or not, once my higher self told me what was around the corner, all sorts of amazing things happened. I always wanted to live next to the beach, for example, and now I do! People I know who have experimented with wish books have found wonderful houses, great boyfriends, trips to America and all kinds of great things, just by tuning into their 'destiny road map' and seeing which wishes are close enough to touch.

So now you know that the things you secretly long for are within your reach. You just need to establish what they are and make the right choices along the way. It's amazing what you can accomplish if you really, really want to. Use your psychic skills for the good of all and always be practical about what you want to achieve. The future looks bright – make sure you sparkle in it!

CHAPTER FIVE

How to see your aura

Professional psychics work with their chakras and aura in their own psychic gym. You can do it too, but first, you need to understand what a chakra (pronounced 'shark-rah') and an aura ('orr-ah') actually is.

We all have seven coloured lights going from the top of our head down to the bottom of our back. These lights are psychic energy centres. To do powerful psychic work, you need to imagine them being filled with even more colour and light than usual. Then, at the end, you imagine switching off the lights, so that you can return to normal and get on with your life. Otherwise you'd be powerfully psychic all the time, and that can get in the way of everything!

The Christmas tree meditation

Meditation is a big part of the psychic gym and in a minute you'll read about a special meditation you can do every day to make yourself more psychic. But what about when you want to give yourself an extra blast? For that, you'll need to try the Christmas tree meditation.

First, shut the door ...

 Close the door so you won't be disturbed and turn off your mobile phone. Next, sit on a chair, or on the edge of the bed, with your feet flat on the floor, and your hands palms-down on the tops of your legs. Now, imagine that you are a Christmas tree. It shouldn't be hard – no matter what time of year it is, you can instantly picture a nice green Christmas tree with a brown trunk, and lots of lights and decorations. Now, surround yourself with a balloon of white light.

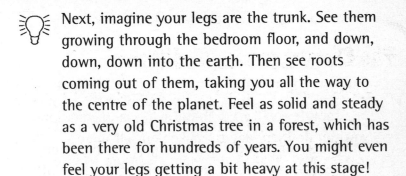

Next, imagine your legs are the trunk. See them growing through the bedroom floor, and down, down, down into the earth. Then see roots coming out of them, taking you all the way to the centre of the planet. Feel as solid and steady as a very old Christmas tree in a forest, which has been there for hundreds of years. You might even feel your legs getting a bit heavy at this stage!

Next, imagine that you have seven layers of beautiful fairy lights stretching across you. At the top, which is the top of your head, you have glittery gold lights. In your mind, make them brighter.

Now, move down to your throat and neck. You have sparkly purple and blue lights here. Once again, imagine turning them up, and making them dazzling.

By now the top of you should be nicely lit up, just like a Christmas tree in a window. So move down to your heart, and picture twinkling green lights. Make them very strong and powerful, and then move down your body again, to the bit just below your heart. See that as a lot of dazzling yellow lights.

 Still here? You might be feeling a little bit light yourself by now, as you are doing what psychics call 'charging' your chakras. After the yellow lights, see some bright orange lights around your belly button area. And finally, right at the base of your spine, where your bottom is on the chair, or on the bed, see amazing bright red lights – brighter and more powerful than any traffic light!

 Congratulations! Your chakras are now charged. And you are in the right state to do your very best psychic work (any of the experiments in this book would be ideal). Just do the Christmas tree exercise whenever you feel you need extra super psychic energy.

★★ SWITCHING OFF!

Switching off is important too. If you leave a
Christmas tree on all the time, eventually the
bulbs in the fairy lights pop, or sometimes the
wires can even short-circuit. The chakras also need
special care, so once you have finished doing your
big psychic charge, make sure you switch off.
Start from the bottom of your Christmas tree, and
steadily turn off the red, orange, yellow, green,
blue, purple and gold lights. You might feel
yourself breathing out with a huge 'aaaah' once
you have done this. You will probably feel very
calm and settled. You are now closed down, and
back to normal.

The aura

Just like a chicken in an egg, we humans have an egg of energy around us. It is made up of light, and it helps keep us safe and sound. This is very important when you do psychic work, as you are much more sensitive than normal, and you really will need your 'egg' around you.

Have you ever seen your aura? Professional psychics see it around people and animals all the time, and even around light bulbs and street lights. It looks like fuzzy coloured lights. And yes, it really does look like an egg – a sort of big balloon of light that fits right around your body, and over the top of your head.

To see your aura, look in the bedroom mirror at night. A normal electric light bulb can help you to see it. Just sit or stand one metre away, and relax. Don't try too hard or it might not work! Look around the top of your head, around the tops of your shoulders, and even around your ears. In a few minutes, you should be able to see a line of white light which goes right around your head and shoulders. If it's a full length mirror, you may even see the light going down over your legs as well. If you keep looking, you might start to see colours. Congratulations! It's your aura. It's your magical mysterious energy field and it's important to look after it.

✦✦ CLEANING YOUR AURA

It's good to clean your aura every now and then. Just like a proper eggshell, it can get 'dirty' with other people's bad moods, or even from brushing up against too many other auras in a crowd. Have you ever been out shopping, or at a concert, or on holiday at the beach, and been crammed up against hundreds of other people? If you felt VERY tired afterwards then your aura was probably picking up 'psychic dirt' from others.

To clean it up, once again sit down on the chair, or on the bed, with your palms flat on top of your thighs. Now, imagine that you are sitting on a rock underneath a waterfall. It's a huge, beautiful waterfall, full of sparkling light inside the water. Feel it pouring down on top of your head, splashing over your shoulders, and washing every part of you, even your feet! Do this for ten minutes. Tell yourself that this imaginary waterfall is cleaning your aura, and guess what? It will!

★ ★ CHARGING YOUR AURA

Now that you're clean, you need to put extra energy and power back into your aura. You do this simply by feeling the white light egg around you become brighter, and brighter. Really 'see' it in your mind's eye. And know that this egg has a very powerful shell. Nothing can get in or out unless you say so.

✶✶ USING THE PSYCHIC GYM

If you do these exercises every other day, you will soon notice the effects. However, even if you only remember to do them once a month, you should still get better results as a psychic once you use your gym. Well – it's easier than getting on an exercise bike anyway! A good psychic is one who uses her powers wisely and doesn't lose touch with the real world. A healthy, balanced lifestyle will ensure that you keep your wits about you and keep you happy, safe and alert.

CHAPTER SIX

Your hidden past lives

Past lives and your Life's Fate

Do you believe in past lives? Many children and young people do, probably because they are better at remembering them than adults are. (The older you get, the harder it is to recall who you were last time round.)

Whether you believe or not, there is some interesting evidence to suggest that young people know more about other cultures, and countries, and periods in history, than their teachers and parents would expect. In some experiments, children as young as nine have been shown hundreds of Japanese words, and asked to pick out which bits were poems. Amazingly, although the children didn't know Japanese, they sorted out the poems from the dummy words. His Holiness The Dalai Lama got his job because he recognized objects belonging to the previous Dalai Lama, who the Tibetans say was him in a previous life – that's why he knew what was 'his' and what wasn't.

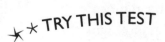TRY THIS TEST

You will need to get a friend to read the following bits aloud, while you are lying on the bed in the relaxed way you learned about on pages 32–33. Go through the tightening and relaxing exercise, and then listen to what your friend is telling you, and shut your eyes. When you have finished, tell your friend what happened to you, then let her take her turn.

'This experiment will show you who you were in a past life. First of all, please imagine that you are on a beautiful beach. You have bare feet. You can feel the sun on your face, and the sand between your toes. You can hear the waves too,

making a swishing sound. Nobody else
is around except you. As you walk along
the edge of the blue water, you can see
pink and white shells on the sand. As
you look up, you see blue skies, and fluffy white
clouds. As you look down, you see the golden
sand, and the shells. There is nobody to the left of
you, and nobody to the right of you. Just the sea
on one side, and some tall cliffs on the other. For
the next five minutes, walk along the beach,
admiring the sea, and the shells, and enjoy the
feeling of your feet in the water, as you paddle
and walk at the same time.'

Wait five minutes!

'You have now walked quite a long way, and you
are ready for a rest. Looking at the cliffs alongside
the beach, you notice a green door in one of
them. You walk over to the door, and see that it
has a beautiful green crystal doorknob, that
sparkles in the sunlight. You turn the doorknob,
open the door, and walk in. You are in a room full
of white light, with a white floor, and white walls.

Now, look down at your feet. You are wearing shoes. What kind of shoes are they? These are the shoes you wore in a past life. Look at your legs. Are you a man or a woman? A boy or a girl? Are your legs bare, or are you wearing something over them? Look at your hands. What sort of hands are they? Are you wearing jewellery? Are your hands clean or dirty? Are you wearing gloves, or nothing at all? Are your nails short or long? Notice your skin. Is it black, white, brown, or another colour? Take five minutes to really look at yourself and what you look like, in this special white room, because this is the way you once were.'

Wait five minutes!

'I only have three questions left to ask you. What is your name? What is your favourite food? And what have you done today?'

Wait one minute!

'Please leave the white room by using the green door. Now you are back on the beach again. And

it is time to wake up and come back to the room.
Squeeze your fingers and toes, stretch yourself,
and become aware of yourself, lying on the bed,
listening to me. Now, open your eyes and tell me
everything before we write it down!'

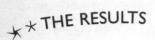 ## THE RESULTS

Were you surprised by what you saw? Most people
are amazed by the shoes they have on their feet
(although some people realize they are not
wearing any shoes at all, and have quite dirty
feet, with lots of cuts and bruises). These shoes,
or bare feet, are your first clue to your past life.
Your clothes, the food you like to eat, your name,
and even what you 'did' that day, in your past
life, are the other clues you need to discover who
you once were.

   If you're not sure, show your teacher what you
have written down, as he or she may be able to

spot if your shoes or name were foreign,
or from centuries ago, or even millennia
ago! Then it's up to you to raid as many

books from the library as you can, so you can find out exactly what country and time you might have come from, in your past life. Were you a man or a woman? Don't be too shocked if you were a man! It's very common for people to choose their Life's Fate as the opposite sex, because they want to learn what it's like to experience everything from the opposite point of view. Perhaps you were a boy in a past life and just wanted to come back as a girl!

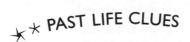

✦✦ PAST LIFE CLUES

Every time you visit a museum or place of historical interest, see if any of the exhibits give you a funny feeling of familiarity. Do you know something about the objects you are looking at before you read the information sheet next to the glass case? Does anything give you a strange sensation that you have seen it before? Do you get goosebumps when you look at something? Pay attention – these may be past life clues.

Hopefully by now you're realizing that that your past, present and future are all linked. Whether you believe in past lives or not the experiment in this chapter is a fun way to think outside your everyday experiences. And you might just find out something extraordinary about yourself ...

CHAPTER SEVEN

Mysterious twists of fate

In the previous example on page 48 you learned a bit more about fate and free will, and how they work together (like when it's your fate to marry a man in another country, but you get to choose the way in which you'll end up in his home town). It's also important to remember that our Life's Fate is created by TWISTS of fate. These are events beyond your control (like your family moving, or your Mum getting pregnant, or your Dad changing jobs, or even your parents splitting up). Each event creates lots of other little events that spring off it – and these can create your Life's Fate.

For example, if you were good at dancing in your past life (perhaps you were in the Bolshoi Ballet in Russia) you might find your Dad

gets a new job in a new city, where there is a very
good ballet school – right next door to your
house. You might make friends with a girl who
lives nearby, and because she's in a dance class,
you go too. Soon, you end up winning
prizes for your dancing, and before too
long, you find you've won a dance
scholarship – to Russia! This is a very
good example of a chain of fate, or a series of
twists of fate.

Think about your life for a minute, and all the
stuff that's happened to you so far. Do you think
you can see a chain of fate, or a few twists of
fate along the way?

Twists of fate are seen psychically, along with
your Life's Fate. That's why psychics can
sometimes make predictions ten or twenty years
ahead into the future. When I was 23 years
old, I saw a psychic who told me that after
the age of 30 I would never stop travelling.
At the time, I thought this couldn't be true,
because I couldn't afford to fly anywhere – and I
didn't really want to anyway! However, it was my
Life's Fate to travel a lot, on behalf of a charity
called War Child, so sure enough, after I turned

30 I spent several years flying between
Europe, America, Asia and Australia.

Your Life's Fate is something you
don't have much choice about. Sometimes it's
because you can't say no! For example, if a
gorgeous boy asks you out, and you've had a
crush on him all year, of COURSE you're going to
say yes. If he is part of your Life's Fate, then your
relationship takes off because you really, really
want it to. At other times, your Life's Fate is in
the hands of other people (like your teachers,
or your family) and you don't have much say in
what happens.

What about free will, though? Can you predict
free will as well as the Life's Fate bits? The answer
is yes, but first of all you have to understand what
free will is. We've talked a bit about it on page 48
but here's a fuller explanation.

Yes or no?

Free will is about making yes or no choices. Will
you go on a school trip overseas, or will you end
up staying at home? Will you go to a school party

with your best friend, or a boy that you like? Will you buy your Dad a pair of socks for Christmas, or will you be creative and make him a sunglasses case instead?

Because your free will is at work, psychics can't predict what you'll do. But they CAN predict the choice that will be ahead of you, and even how you'll feel about that choice. This is what's known as a Fork in the Road reading. And here's how you can do it ...

★ ★ THE BIG FATE AND FREE WILL EXPERIMENT

By now you should be a bit of an expert on fate and free will. You will need to understand them if you're going to be a true psychic – and also if you're going to be able to do this experiment. The results should astound and amaze you. And best of all, you'll learn all about the mysterious way that destiny can operate.

Forks in the road

What will your forks in the road be next month? To find out, get a large sheet of white card, and with a ruler, make 12 squares which you then cut out with a pair of scissors. Using a felt-tip pen, on the front of each card, write one of these categories:

HAIR AND CLOTHES

SHOPPING AND MONEY

PHONES AND EMAIL

HOME AND FAMILY

TALENTS AND HOBBIES

HEALTH AND FITNESS

BOYS AND LOVE

GHOSTS AND SPIRITS

HOLIDAYS AND FOREIGNERS

SCHOOL AND SUCCESS

FRIENDS AND GROUPS

SECRETS AND DREAMS

Make a pile of the cards so that you can't see what's written on them. Shuffle them around on the table, mixing them all up, putting them in a neat pile at the end. By now you should have absolutely no idea which card says what thing!

Now, open your psychic centre. This is done by visualizing white light all around you, and then breathing white light into the bit just above your belly button. This is the solar plexus chakra and it's your psychic headquarters!

Keep on breathing like this for a few minutes until you become aware of the bit above your belly button – it may be twitchy, or tickly, or feel heavier than usual. It may even feel as if you've swallowed a whole packet of sweets and that's where it's ended up.

Now say out loud, 'I ask the Universe to help me help myself. What big choice do I face next month? Where will my fork in the road be?'

Then take just one card out of the 12, and turn it over. What have you got? This tells you the areas of life where you will be facing a big yes or no decision.

Psychic guidance

Sometimes forks in the road can be extremely confusing. Take Megan, for example, whose card was all about boys and love. Sure enough, when the following month arrived, she had to choose whether to be nice to Andrew, even though she knew he secretly liked her, or not to be so friendly so he didn't get the wrong idea. She secretly liked Graham, another boy, who was popular with all the girls at school – so should she keep on hanging around Andrew after class or not? Megan liked having a boy who was interested in her, but at the same time she didn't want to lead Andrew on. Aaargh! What's a girl to do? This is where psychic guidance came in. Megan used it, and you can use it too.

✦✦ GUIDANCE CARDS

Take another sheet of white card, as Megan did, and divide it up into 12 squares again. On one side of each card, write the following words of guidance:

CONFIDENCE
CARING
COMMUNICATION
LOVE
ACTION
OPPORTUNITY
COMMON SENSE
NEW THINGS
KINDNESS
CHANGE
HARD WORK
EASY WORK

Surround yourself with white light, and start breathing some of the white light into your solar plexus chakra again, so you can really feel it above your belly button. Now say out loud, 'Dear Universe, please give me some psychic guidance about my fork in the road. What one thing do I need to think about, that will give me the answer?' Finish with the golden psychic rule: 'For the highest good of all!'

Pick a card. Look at your answer. If it's
CONFIDENCE, for example, decide yes or no on
the basis of what will make you feel most
confident – feeling sure of yourself, and feeling
good about yourself – and what will make others
feel truly confident too. What about CARING?
That's easy! Which fork in the road should you
take to be most caring in this situation?
COMMUNICATION is not just about talking, it's
also about texting, emailing and writing
letters. If you get this card, your psychic
guidance wants you to think about that,
more than anything else. Which choice is best for
 communication? The LOVE card doesn't
come up very often, but when it does,
people get all excited. It's not just about
love between boys and girls, though – it's also
about the love you have for friends, family and
even pets. Which choice is most loving? You can
use the rest of the cards in the same way:

⭐ ACTION: Which choice would let you take
action?

⭐ OPPORTUNITY: Which choice spells
opportunity?

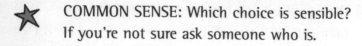

★ COMMON SENSE: Which choice is sensible? If you're not sure ask someone who is.

★ NEW THINGS: Which choice would let you try something new?

★ KINDNESS: Which choice is kindest?

★ CHANGE: Which choice would let you make a big change?

★ HARD WORK: Which choice is hard work, but worth it?

★ EASY WORK: Which choice is easy work – in other words, you won't have to try?

In this example, Megan picked up the OPPORTUNITY card. The choice that would give her the most opportunity in life was definitely spending more time with Andrew and getting to know him properly. This is exactly what Megan did, and after being friends for a while with Andrew, she realized she didn't fancy Graham so much after all (he had too many girls running after him for a start). After a few months, it was Andrew she felt weak at the knees about! He felt the same way, so he asked her out, and her opportunity was fulfilled.

⋆

Cosmic clues and signs

Don't just go on your divine guidance cards though. Look for clues and signs as well. Is a good friend or relative whom you trust giving you the same advice as the card? Have you just seen a TV programme which is all about the same thing you are going through? Have you just borrowed a library book which has a heroine just like you, facing a similar choice? The cosmos is a mysterious and powerful thing. So trust the universe, because it will always give you clues and signs. These will help ADD to your cards and let you know that you are on the right track. Using the cards is a great way to help your psychic gym routine, by the way. Try them weekly, and score yourself over a month. The more you use them, the better they will work for you.

✦ MAKE AN ANSWER FEATHER

Native Americans use Answer Feathers to find solutions to choices which are puzzling them. All you need to do is find a good pigeon, seagull or other bird feather. Make sure it's clean! Keep it safe in an envelope with your name on it. Say out loud, 'Dear Universe, please charge this feather as my Answer Feather, so I can help myself and help others find good and useful answers.' Then keep it with you all day, until your answer appears. Remember, you can use this feather again. Just put it away safely for next time. Don't use it too often though – it's best saved up for special problems. But it is an excellent way to get the cosmic clues and signs that we've just been talking about.

⭒⭒ CLOSING DOWN

Just as TV stations close down their transmission, when you have been doing any psychic work with your belly-button area (your psychic centre) you also need to close down. This is easy. Just picture a white light around this area of your body growing smaller and smaller, until it's just a tiny dot. Then say to yourself, 'I am now closed down.' That's it – your psychic work is finished! Many psychics like to pretend they are in a white sleeping bag, and pull the zip up, right up to their chin, and tie the hood over their hair. You might like to do this too, especially as it protects your aura.

✦✦ AND DON'T FORGET ...

The life you build in this life (how you shape your Life's Fate) can determine what kind of future life you have too. So if you want a past life from the 21st century you'll be happy about in the 22nd century, then you'd better get a move on and make it happen! You're the one in charge here – you have the power to make decisions about your life and how you live it. There are so many exciting opportunities ahead and lots of choices to make. Your intuition is a great tool for making decisions as it often highlights things that your psychic self wants you to pay attention to. See how your life shapes up and enjoy the ride!

CHAPTER EIGHT

Be a super psychic!

How to meditate

To be a super psychic, you need to meditate every day. It shouldn't take you long – just ten minutes in the morning and ten minutes in the evening. Meditating not only gives you a sense of peace and calm, it also helps you live your life with ALL your senses – not just five of them. This makes everything easier, from getting your hair cut, to talking to boys. So here's how to begin. First of all, you'll need to make sure your clothing isn't too tight, and that your shoes and socks are off (if it's cold, though, keep a pair of soft fluffy socks ON).

Now, with the door closed, and the phone
switched off, sit on the floor, either cross-legged
(if you can manage it) or with your legs straight
out in front of you. Keep your back very straight,
 and your head up, as if there is an
invisible piece of cotton being pulled
from your scalp up towards the clouds.
Start breathing from the lower part of your
tummy – the bit beneath your belly button. Most
people breathe too high, so that they are inhaling
and exhaling from ABOVE the belly button line.
But your best breath is very deep and comes right
up from the lower half of your body.

As you breathe from below your belly button,
close your eyes, and imagine a flame of white
light travelling up, past your heart, chest, throat,
up past the middle spot between your eyebrows,
and out through the top of your head. See it
travelling as you breathe in. This white light might
travel very fast from bottom to top, in three
seconds – or as your breathing slows down, it
might take up to 10 seconds to reach the top.

Concentrate on this light, breathing it
in from the bottom of your body and out
through the top – and try to really see it.

Thoughts will pop in and out of your head as you do this. Don't pay them much attention. Just let them go, like clouds skimming across the sky. Say to yourself, 'Oh, there goes another thought,' and then return to focusing on your breathing, and seeing the white light.

Pretty soon, you should be able to see a lot of space out there ... even with your eyes closed. You may feel as if you are seeing around a vast galaxy of blackness – or you might feel as if your head has become bigger! (Don't worry, it hasn't!)

Remain in this space for as long as you can – ten minutes is ideal, but if you want to meditate for any longer, do make sure you set an alarm clock or an egg timer.

When it's time to come back to the real world, shake yourself around a bit, and have a glass of water. Do you feel calmer? You should do. And most importantly, if you can do this everyday, twice a day, you will be developing all your senses, so that you are well on your way to being a super psychic!

Meditating isn't hard but it does take practice. Try using it as part of your psychic gym routine and try it just a bit at a time in the same way you might practise push-ups very gently at first. Don't give up if you get bored or restless. Just keep going! Meditation is very safe and relaxing and you may fall asleep if you try it just once or twice: persist, though, and you'll find that with practice you'll become an expert and that your psychic powers increase.

Searching for answers

Once you are used to meditating, try the Magic Encyclopaedia Meditation to seek answers to your problems, or your questions. Here are some typical things that people ask, by the way!

 What should I be when I grow up?

 How can I stop someone saying nasty things about me?

How can I get the boy I like to ask me to the school dance?

 Will I have a nice time if I go on the school trip?

You are bound to have a few of your own, but when you do the Magic Encyclopaedia Meditation, it helps to ask the question as follows ...

First, say out loud your real question (for example, 'Will I have a nice time if I go on the school trip?'). And after that, say this: 'Please tell me the number one thing I need to think about, to answer my question.' Try it now if you like. Say out loud what your question is, then add the next line.

✦✦ NOW CLOSE YOUR EYES

Now that you have practised the question, close
your eyes. This time, after you have done ten
minutes of breathing the white light up through
your body and out through the top of your head,
imagine that you are in a beautiful library. There
are millions of books on millions of shelves – and
it's so enormous that you can't see all the way
round it. The books are all colours, shapes and
sizes, and they are all on different kinds of
subjects. Let yourself walk around the library for a
while, in your imagination, until you come to one
particular shelf, and one particular book: your
Magic Encyclopaedia!

Your psychic self will know exactly where to look,
by the way, so don't worry about finding it. Now,
once the book is in front of you, take it off the
shelf, flick through it, and turn to a page
somewhere in the middle. On this page is a
drawing, or a message. What is it? Try and

remember it! This is the answer to your question, and it has been in your Magic Encyclopaedia all along.

★ ★ TRUE STORIES

Here are some true stories from super psychic people who have tried the Magic Encyclopaedia Meditation.

 BETHIA asked, 'Will I get some money if I sell the cards that I've been making? Please tell me the number one thing I need to think about, to answer my question.' The Magic Encyclopaedia showed her a picture of a tourist shop near her home. She went in there and they bought five of her cards on the spot.

 GEMMA asked, 'Will my brother get better? Please tell me the number one thing I need to think about, to answer my question.' (He had been in hospital for some time.) The Magic Encyclopaedia showed her the word TIME with a picture of a

clock. She thought this meant that she would
need to be patient, and she was right – in time,
her brother did get well again.

 CORY asked, 'Does Bethia like me? Please tell me
the number one thing I need to think about, to
answer my question.' In his Encyclopaedia, he saw
the name of another boy in their class. This boy
was very shy and quiet, but Cory realized that
Bethia might secretly like him. So he asked her –
and she did!

★ ★ COMING BACK DOWN TO EARTH

Once you have finished the Magic Encyclopaedia
Meditation, it's very important to come back
down to earth (or you could be stuck in the
library forever!). Open your eyes, shake yourself,
and plant both feet on the ground. Feel the earth
under your feet, and have a glass of water.
Surround yourself with a bubble of white light,
too, so that your egg (your aura) is nice and

comfortable. Then do something normal, like watching TV or reading a book.

Like anything new and demanding, you should try meditating only a bit at first. This will help you to build up your psychic strength. The more you practise the better a psychic you will be. The psychic exercises in this book are meant to be fun and a good way to find out more about yourself and your friends. And they're a great way to boost your chances of success and happiness in life.

CHAPTER NINE

Fairies, angels and spirit guides

As you get used to working with the mysterious invisible world of auras, telepathy, colour power, meditation, past lives – and all the other weird and wonderful things you have read about so far – you might be ready to take the next step.

Just as the ocean is hidden from view for most of the time (but it's packed with life) the spirit world is also extremely lively and busy. Yet for most of us, it doesn't seem to exist at all. Oh, you might hear stories from people who claim to have seen a ghost, but what about the fairies who inhabit certain gardens or special stretches of woodland? What about angels, who can make the most incredible things happen in the blink of an eye? And what about spirit guides, who are wise old souls who lived many years before, and have now chosen to help and guide us over here in the real world?

Second sight – myth or reality?

Second sight is another way of saying that your 'clair' senses are very strong. It means you can actually see (or even photograph) fairies, angels and spirit guides. This is very difficult for most people – and unless you have seen aspects of the spiritual world since you were a child, it may never happen to you at all. But nevertheless, there are ways to encourage a bit of magic into your life.

★★ ANGELS LOVE PEOPLE WHO ACT LIKE ANGELS!

The more you act as a human angel, the more angelic forces will be attracted to you. The spirit world – the invisible world – is composed of

Fairies at the bottom of the garden

I have a friend called Eugenie who actually leaves sandwiches out for the fairies! I have never gone that far, but I have built a special fairy corner in my garden, in which I have planted mushrooms, and also added beautiful amethyst and rose quartz crystals. You can have fun, too, if you ask your parents for a special part of the garden, or even a windowbox, which you can decorate to attract the fairies. You can grow any tiny plant or herb you like, but do try and find some other pretty things – seashells, or little white stones, or even tiny statues – to put in your fairy corner.

Fairies are very real, particularly to people in Ireland – and I am lucky enough to have photographed some. A fairy queen turned up in my fairy corner one day when I was

photographing the garden. I had no idea she was there until the photograph came back from the developers, but she has a brown crown and clear wings in the middle of the picture.

Try some photography yourself in your fairy corner and see what you can spot. And remember that fairies love to help plants grow – it's their job – so don't be too surprised if the flowers or trees near the fairy corner suddenly zoom up in height. Fairies attract fun, laughter, good times and wonderful people so it's a very good idea to have some in your life. They are getting squashed out of the big cities as we keep on building concrete over the grass and trees, so try wherever you can to create a place which is just for them.

Spirit guides

And, finally, a word about spirit guides. You may already know who your spirit guide is (some girls do) and perhaps you have seen him or her. In other cases, you may never actually come into contact with this wise helper from the spirit world, yet he or she will always be helping you with your Life's Fate!

So far in this book you have learned a little about
the mysterious road map of destiny that is
out there for you. Your guide's job is to keep
you on the right road, so you don't go
wandering off, and he or she will do this in all
kinds of ways. You may have a vivid, powerful,
unforgettable dream one night that seems to tell
you that you must do something, or speak to
someone, or go somewhere – that's your guide,
showing you an answer in your dreams!

Sometimes a wise and wonderful thought
might just pop into your head, when
you are thinking about something else.
That's your guide too – they 'whisper'
to you telepathically when you are
relaxed sometimes, but it's so subtle and gentle
that you may not even realize what has happened
until later.

Guides choose to help us because they have
had so much life experience down here on earth,
and when they pass to the spirit world, they
volunteer to assist us here. They are more down-
to-earth than angels, and they know us better
(because they see all the problems that we have
to struggle with). They have a different energy to

fairies too; fairies are lighter, and brighter, and more interested in the garden, than they are in our big life challenges.

Your guide enjoys always being around, because he or she learns and grows by helping you, so it's a two-way process. Professional psychics work with a team of guides, who help them with their work, and I have a Chinese man and a Native American man who keep me on the right road, and even do useful things like tell me what to put in my books. Believe it or not, this book has been written with my own guides providing useful hints and tips, so I hope you enjoy it. And enjoy your psychic powers, as they are the gateway to a happier life for you and others around you.

Last words

Every country and culture on the planet once had psychic energy woven into their everyday lives. Some of them still do! Scientists are able to prove these psychic powers from time to time, but the real test is your experiments at home. How successful have you been? Can you guess what a friend wants you to know? Do you recognize objects from your past lives? Can you tell what your pet cat is trying to tell you? I'll bet that you've come along way on your psychic journey and have found out all kinds of fascinating things about YOU and your life. Keep up the practice at the psychic gym and you could become an expert!

Remember to use your psychic skills for the good of all and you'll see the results before long. Keep your psychic powers topped up and enjoy this secret part of amazing you.

Index

✳ ✳